WITHDRAWN

SPARKS OF LIFE

Chemical Elements that Make Life Possible

NITROGEN

by

Jean F. Blashfield

RSVP®

RAINTREE
STECK-VAUGHN
PUBLISHERS
A Steck-Vaughn Company

Austin, Texas

Special thanks to our technical consultant,
Jeanne Hamers, Ph.D.,
formerly with the Institute of Chemical Education,
Madison, Wisconsin

Development: Books Two, Delavan, Wisconsin
Graphics: Krueger Graphics, Janesville, Wisconsin
Interior Design: Peg Esposito
Photo Research and Indexing: Margie Benson

Raintree Steck-Vaughn Publisher's Staff:
Publishing Director: Walter Kossmann   Project Editor: Frank Tarsitano
Design Manager: Joyce Spicer   Electronic Production: Scott Melcer

Library of Congress Cataloging-in-Publication Data:
Blashfield, Jean F.
    Nitrogen / by Jean F. Blashfield.
        p.   cm. — (Sparks of life)
    Includes bibliographical references (p.   -   ) and index.
    Summary: Discusses the origin, discovery, special characteristics, and use of
nitrogen in such products as explosives and fertilizers.
    ISBN 0-8172-5039-5
    1. Nitrogen — Juvenile literature.   [1. Nitrogen.]   I. Title.   II. Series:
Blashfield, Jean F.   Sparks of life.
QD181.N1B52   1999   98-4534
548' .711 — dc21   CIP   AC

Printed and bound in the United States
1 2 3 4 5 6 7 8 9 LB 03 02 01 00 99 98

PHOTO CREDITS: Agence France Presse/Corbis-Bettman 50; American Petroleum
Institute 33; Archive Photos 14, 48 left; ©B.I.F.C. cover; CF Industries 35, 37; Corbis
11, 12; CNRI/Science Photo Library 16; FBI 57; ©1991 Stephen Frisch, Stock Boston
cover; GM Media Archives, All Rights Reserved 40; ©Julie Houck, Stock Boston 29;
JLM Visuals 13, 18, 24, 45, 47; ©Greg Johnston/International Stock Photo 53;
Medichrome/Div. The Stock Shop Inc. cover; ©Rudy Tesa/International Stock 48 top;
NASA 22; ©Robert C. Russell, International Stock Photo cover; Tetra Second Nature
52; TRW Safety Systems 54; USDA 42; © M.I. Walker/Photo Researchers 31; ©Nik
Wheeler 39; USDA-ARS Information Staff cover, 25, 27.

CONTENTS

Periodic Table of the Elements

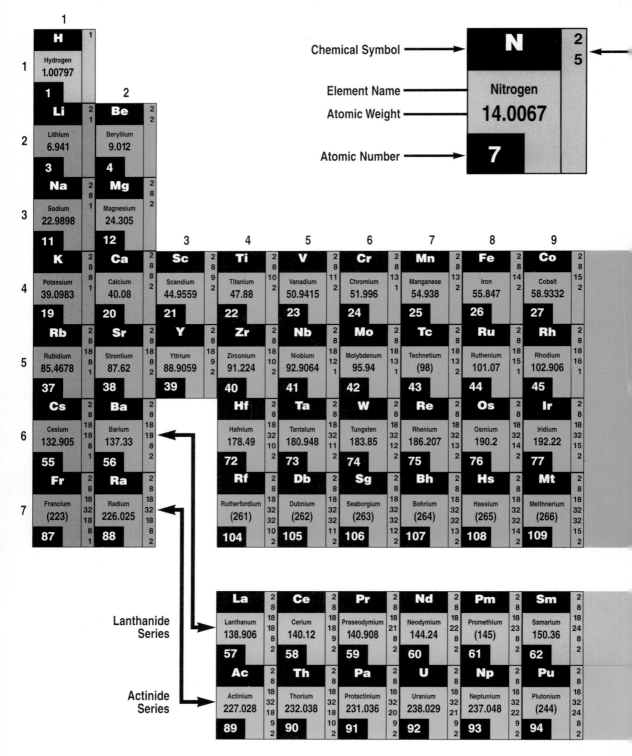

Chemical Symbol → **N** | 2 5

Element Name → Nitrogen
Atomic Weight → 14.0067

Atomic Number → 7

Number of electrons in each shell,
beginning with the K shell, top.

See next page for explanations.

			13	14	15	16	17	18

18

He — Helium — 4.0026 — 2 — (2)

13 — B Boron 10.81 — 5 — (2, 3)
14 — C Carbon 12.011 — 6 — (2, 4)
15 — N Nitrogen 14.0067 — 7 — (2, 5)
16 — O Oxygen 15.9994 — 8 — (2, 6)
17 — F Fluorine 18.9984 — 9 — (2, 7)
18 — Ne Neon 20.179 — 10 — (2, 8)

Al Aluminum 26.9815 — 13 — (2, 8, 3)
Si Silicon 28.0855 — 14 — (2, 8, 4)
P Phosphorus 30.9738 — 15 — (2, 8, 5)
S Sulfur 32.06 — 16 — (2, 8, 6)
Cl Chlorine 35.453 — 17 — (2, 8, 7)
Ar Argon 39.948 — 18 — (2, 8, 8)

10	11	12	13	14	15	16	17	18

Ni Nickel 58.69 — 28 — (2, 8, 16, 2)
Cu Copper 63.546 — 29 — (2, 8, 18, 1)
Zn Zinc 65.39 — 30 — (2, 8, 18, 2)
Ga Gallium 69.72 — 31 — (2, 8, 18, 3)
Ge Germanium 72.59 — 32 — (2, 8, 18, 4)
As Arsenic 74.9216 — 33 — (2, 8, 18, 5)
Se Selenium 78.96 — 34 — (2, 8, 18, 6)
Br Bromine 79.904 — 35 — (2, 8, 18, 7)
Kr Krypton 83.80 — 36 — (2, 8, 18, 8)

Pd Palladium 106.42 — 46 — (2, 8, 18, 18)
Ag Silver 107.868 — 47 — (2, 8, 18, 18, 1)
Cd Cadmium 112.41 — 48 — (2, 8, 18, 18, 2)
In Indium 114.82 — 49 — (2, 8, 18, 18, 3)
Sn Tin 118.71 — 50 — (2, 8, 18, 18, 4)
Sb Antimony 121.75 — 51 — (2, 8, 18, 18, 5)
Te Tellurium 127.6 — 52 — (2, 8, 18, 18, 6)
I Iodine 126.905 — 53 — (2, 8, 18, 18, 7)
Xe Xenon 131.29 — 54 — (2, 8, 18, 18, 8)

Pt Platinum 195.08 — 78 — (2, 8, 18, 32, 17, 1)
Au Gold 196.967 — 79 — (2, 8, 18, 32, 18, 1)
Hg Mercury 200.59 — 80 — (2, 8, 18, 32, 18, 2)
Tl Thallium 204.383 — 81 — (2, 8, 18, 32, 18, 3)
Pb Lead 207.2 — 82 — (2, 8, 18, 32, 18, 4)
Bi Bismuth 208.98 — 83 — (2, 8, 18, 32, 18, 5)
Po Polonium (209) — 84 — (2, 8, 18, 32, 18, 6)
At Astatine (210) — 85 — (2, 8, 18, 32, 18, 7)
Rn Radon (222) — 86 — (2, 8, 18, 32, 18, 8)

(Uun) Ununnilium (269) — 110 — (2, 8, 18, 32, 32, 17, 1)
(Unu) Unununium (272) — 111 — (2, 8, 18, 32, 32, 18, 1)
(Uub) Ununbium (277) — 112 — (2, 8, 18, 32, 32, 18, 2)

Alkali Metals	Transition Metals	Nonmetals	Metalloids	Lanthanide Series
Alkaline Earth Metals	Other Metals	Noble Gases	Actinide Series	**COLOR KEYS**

Eu Europium 151.96 — 63 — (2, 8, 18, 25, 8, 2)
Gd Gadolinium 157.25 — 64 — (2, 8, 18, 25, 9, 2)
Tb Terbium 158.925 — 65 — (2, 8, 18, 27, 8, 2)
Dy Dysprosium 162.50 — 66 — (2, 8, 18, 28, 8, 2)
Ho Holmium 164.93 — 67 — (2, 8, 18, 29, 8, 2)
Er Erbium 167.26 — 68 — (2, 8, 18, 30, 8, 2)
Tm Thulium 168.934 — 69 — (2, 8, 18, 31, 8, 2)
Yb Ytterbium 173.04 — 70 — (2, 8, 18, 32, 8, 2)
Lu Lutetium 174.967 — 71 — (2, 8, 18, 32, 9, 2)

Am Americium (243) — 95 — (2, 8, 18, 32, 25, 8, 2)
Cm Curium (247) — 96 — (2, 8, 18, 32, 25, 9, 2)
Bk Berkelium (247) — 97 — (2, 8, 18, 32, 26, 9, 2)
Cf Californium (251) — 98 — (2, 8, 18, 32, 28, 8, 2)
Es Einsteinium (254) — 99 — (2, 8, 18, 32, 29, 8, 2)
Fm Fermium (257) — 100 — (2, 8, 18, 32, 30, 8, 2)
Md Mendelevium (258) — 101 — (2, 8, 18, 32, 31, 8, 2)
No Nobelium (259) — 102 — (2, 8, 18, 32, 32, 8, 2)
Lr Lawrencium (260) — 103 — (2, 8, 18, 32, 32, 9, 2)

A Guide to the Periodic Table

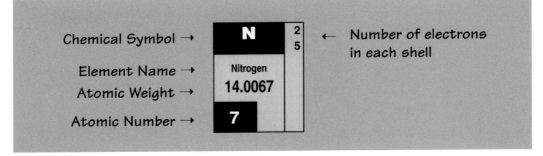

Chemical Symbol →

Element Name →

Atomic Weight →

Atomic Number →

N 2 5 ← Number of electrons in each shell

Nitrogen
14.0067

7

Symbol = an abbreviation of an element name, agreed on by members of the International Union of Pure and Applied Chemistry. The idea to use symbols was started by a Swedish chemist, Jöns Jakob Berzelius, about 1814. Note that the elements with numbers 110, 111, and 112, which were "discovered" in 1996, have not yet been given official names.

Atomic number = the number of protons (particles with a positive charge) in the nucleus of an atom of an element; also equal to the number of electrons (particles with a negative charge) found in the shells, or rings, of an atom that does not have an electrical charge.

Atomic weight = the weight of an element compared to a standard element, carbon. When the Periodic Table was first developed, hydrogen was used as the standard. It was given an atomic weight of 1, but that created some difficulties, and in 1962, the standard was changed to carbon-12, which is the most common form of the element carbon, with an atomic weight of 12.

The Periodic Table on pages 4 and 5 shows the atomic weight of carbon as 12.001 because an atomic weight is an average of the weights, or masses, of all the different naturally occurring forms of an atom. Each form, called an *isotope*, has a different number of neutrons (uncharged particles) in the nucleus. Most elements have several isotopes, but chemists assume that any two samples of an element are made up of the same mixture of isotopes and thus have the same mass, or weight.

Electron shells = regions surrounding the nucleus of an atom in which the electrons move. Historically, electron shells have been described as orbits similar to a planet's orbit. But actually they are whole areas with a specific range of energy levels, in which certain electrons vibrate and move around. The shell closest to the nucleus, the K shell, can contain only 2 electrons. The K shell has the lowest energy level, and it is very hard to break its electrons away. The second shell, L, can contain only 8 electrons. Other shells may contain as many as 32 electrons. The outer shell, in which chemical reactions occur, is called the valence shell.

Periods = horizontal rows of elements in the Periodic Table. A period contains all the elements with the same number of orbital shells of electrons. Note that the actinide and lanthanide (or rare earth) elements shown in rows below the main table really belong within the table, but it is not regarded as practical to print such a wide table as would be required.

Groups = vertical columns of elements in the Periodic Table; also called families. A group contains all elements that naturally have the same number of electrons in the outermost shell or orbital of the atom. Elements in a group tend to behave in similar ways.

Group 1 = *alkali metals*: very reactive and never found in nature in their pure form. Bright, soft metals, they have one valence electron and conduct both electricity and heat.

Group 2 = *alkaline earth metals*: also very reactive and thus do not occur in pure form in nature. Harder and denser than alkali metals, they have two valence electrons that easily combine with other chemicals.

Groups 3–12 = *transition metals*: the great majority of metals, with a variable number of electrons; can exist in pure form.

Groups 13–17 = *metalloids, nonmetals,* and *other transitional metals.* Metalloids possess some characteristics of metals and some of nonmetals. Unlike metals and metalloids, nonmetals do not conduct electricity

Group 18 = *noble,* or *rare, gases*: in general, these nonmetallic gaseous elements do not react with other elements because their valence shells are full.

AIR, LIFE, AND ALCHEMY

Nitrogen has been described as a "schizophrenic" element, meaning that it has several quite different personalities. Pure colorless nitrogen gas in the air we breathe is harmless. Several of its compounds with oxygen, called nitrogen oxides, are pollutants that damage our breathing. As a fertilizer, it helps feed the world. But in the same compounds, it can be made to explode violently.

The Nitrogen Atom

Nitrogen has the chemical symbol N. It is the thirty-third element in abundance in Earth's crust. A nitrogen atom has seven protons (positively charged particles in the nucleus) and seven electrons (negatively charged particles moving around outside the nucleus), giving it an atomic number of 7. Nitrogen has two shells outside the nucleus in which its electrons move. The inner shell contains two electrons and the outer shell has five. Because a nitrogen atom's second, or outer, shell can normally hold eight electrons, the atom can bond, or unite, with three electrons from other atoms.

In the pungent-smelling chemical called ammonia (NH_3), for example, nitrogen bonds with the single electron of each of three hydrogen (H, element #1) atoms. Ammonia gas has such a powerful odor that it can revive a fainting person. Ammonia is also one of the most important chemicals produced by the chemical industry because it is used as a fertilizer that encourages crop growth and helps feed the people of the world.

In the Periodic Table on pages 4 and 5, nitrogen is at the top of the vertical column called Group 15. This group includes elements with room for three more electrons in their outer shells. Other elements in this group are phosphorus (P, element #15), arsenic (As, #33), antimony (Sb, #51), and bismuth (Bi, #83).

Nitrogen's atomic weight is 14.0067. Most nitrogen atoms have fourteen particles (seven neutrons and seven protons) in their nuclei. However, nitrogen-15, another form, or isotope, of nitrogen, has eight neutrons in its nucleus instead of the usual seven. Out of every 1,000 nitrogen atoms, only 4 are nitrogen-15, which gives nitrogen as a whole an atomic weight of 14.0067.

Bonds and Reactions

Some elements exist in their natural state as molecules of two atoms. These are diatomic, meaning two-atom, elements. The nitrogen gas that makes up more than 78 percent of the air we breathe is diatomic. It is written as N_2.

The two atoms of N_2 (also called dinitrogen) are held together by a triple bond. That means that each nitrogen atom shares three electrons with the other atom. This triple bond is

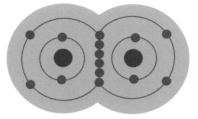

Nitrogen exists as a gas in diatomic molecules. It takes two nitrogen atoms sharing three pairs of electrons to complete each atom's outer electron shell.

very strong, making nitrogen molecules quite inert, or unlikely to react with other atoms.

Because of its relative inertness, nitrogen gas is often used to protect other substances that must not be allowed to react with chemicals around them, especially oxygen (O, element #8). For example, nitrogen is often used in scientific laboratories to coat chemical or biological samples to keep them unchanged.

Under the proper conditions, however, nitrogen atoms can react with other elements. Like carbon (C, element #6), nitrogen can form double bonds. Such bonds are shown in structural formulas. Structural formulas show the relative positions of atoms in a molecule and the bonds between them. The double bond in a nitrogen compound is shown by a double line, usually between a nitrogen atom and a carbon atom. The double bond means that atoms of the two elements share four electrons instead of the usual two. However, nitrogen can also triple-bond with carbon. That's what it does in hydrogen cyanide, or hydrocyanic acid. The structural formula of this devastating poison is:

$$H—C\equiv N$$

Nitrogen by itself is not essential to life, but the compounds it forms in living things are the essence of life itself. Nitrogen is an important part of proteins, the chemicals we need to live, and it also is part of the chemical called DNA, which passes genetic information from generation to generation. Nitrogen is part of every cell in our bodies.

However, nitrogen is virtually nonexistent in the rocks of Earth's crust. Most of the nitrogen that does exist in the crust is in the mineral called saltpeter, which means "saltrock." Saltpeter, also called *niter*, may be found as a nitrate of sodium (Na, element #11), potassium (K, #19), or calcium (Ca, #20).

Investigating Air

Probably the earliest use by alchemists (early chemists who mixed science, magic, and religion) of a nitrogen compound was in nitric acid (HNO_3). The alchemists called nitric acid *aqua fortis*, meaning "strong water," because it corrodes, or eats away, most metals. When mixed with hydrochloric acid (HCl), nitric acid makes *aqua regia* ("royal water"). Aqua regia will dissolve even gold, the "royal" metal.

Joseph Black

The discovery of nitrogen as an element was delayed by a misunderstanding of the nature of air. Many alchemists believed that a burning substance gave off an invisible material which they called phlogiston, meaning "able to be burned." It was thought that the only role air played in burning was as a means for the phlogiston to leave the burning substance.

Scottish chemist Joseph Black tried in the 1750s to find out what gases air contained. He removed the oxygen from an enclosed volume of air by burning something in it. The burning, or combustion, removed oxygen from air by combining it with carbon to form carbon dioxide (CO_2). He then passed the modified air through a chemical that absorbed the CO_2. What remained of the original air sample was mostly nitrogen. However, Black did not know exactly what he had.

Eighteenth-century English scientist
Henry Cavendish

One of Black's pupils, Daniel Rutherford, at his teacher's suggestion, experimented with what remained of the "air." Rutherford found that a small animal could not live in the "air," nor could the "air" support combustion. He thought the invisible gas must contain all the phlogiston it could hold. He called the gas "phlogisticated air" and announced its discovery in 1772. Rutherford is credited with discovering nitrogen, but his phlogisticated air was not pure nitrogen, nor did he think he had found an element.

Swedish chemist Karl Wilhelm Scheele proposed that air was made up of two main gases. One he called "fire air" because things burned in it. It would later be called oxygen. The other, which would come to be identified as nitrogen, he called "foul" or "spoiled" air.

French chemist Antoine Lavoisier called the spoiled air *azote,* meaning "lifeless," because it could not support life. Today, the French still call nitrogen *azote,* and give it the chemical symbol Az, but most of the world calls the element nitrogen, after the name suggested by another French chemist, Jean Chaptal. However, the name *azote* is seen around the world in such terms as "azide" and "azo," both of which are nitrogen-containing groups in molecules of various nitrogen compounds. In German, nitrogen is called *Stickstoff,* which means "choking material."

English scientist Henry Cavendish also experimented with air. Like Rutherford, he saw that what was left of air after removing oxygen did not support life or burning. In 1785, he was able to separate out carbon dioxide. He called the carbon dioxide gas "mephitic," meaning "foul" air. He thought that the remainder was air that had united with phlogiston. This substance, which he called "noxious air," was primarily nitrogen.

Cavendish tried to get rid of the noxious air (nitrogen) by making it combine with other elements, but the nitrogen was too inert. When he introduced an electric spark, however, the nitrogen combined with oxygen in the air as nitrogen oxide, which he removed. All that remained of the original sample of air was a tiny amount of an even more inert gas he couldn't identify.

It wasn't until 1894 that English physicist Robert John Strutt (Lord Rayleigh) investigated what Cavendish's leftover air actually was. A new instrument had been invented that showed what elements were in a chemical by analyzing the light they gave off when the chemical was burned.

Rayleigh's assistant, William Ramsay, used the new apparatus, called a spectroscope, on the last bit of air. He found that it contained another unidentified substance that could not be broken down further. Ramsay and Rayleigh called the element argon (Ar, element #18), from the Greek word for "inert."

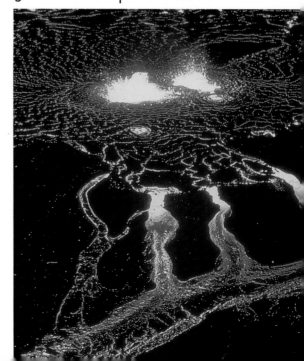

A volcano erupts, spewing lava and gases from deep in the earth.

Where Nitrogen is Found

Theory holds that volcanic eruptions early in our planet's history spewed ammonia gas out of the Earth into the atmosphere. Sunlight then caused hydrogen atoms to separate from the ammonia molecules. The individual nitrogen atoms from the ammonia then united, making diatomic nitrogen. The hydrogen from the ammonia reacted with other elements as part of the planet's solid rocks, whereas the relatively inert nitrogen accumulated in the gaseous atmosphere.

For a time, Earth's atmosphere consisted almost entirely of ammonia and nitrogen. As living things evolved, however, they broke down the ammonia into more nitrogen and hydrogen. Today, Earth's atmosphere near the planet's surface consists of more than 78 percent diatomic nitrogen.

The Oxides

Molecules containing both nitrogen and oxygen are important factors—both useful and harmful—in all life on Earth. Together, these molecules are often referred to as NO_x. The simplest such compound is nitrogen monoxide, with the formula NO. It is colorless, but when NO reacts with oxygen in the air to make nitrogen dioxide (NO_2), it becomes a yellowish-brown gas.

Another important nitrogen oxide is colorless N_2O, dinitrogen monoxide, more commonly known as nitrous oxide. Joseph Priestley discovered nitrous oxide in 1772. Eight years later, twenty-year-old Humphry Davy, a pharmacist's assistant, investigated the ability of the gas to make people relax and sleep. In low concentrations, the gas caused a person who breathed it to lose inhibitions and to readily laugh and cry and generally act silly.

Humphry Davy, British chemist

Inhaling the new "laughing gas" became a popular fad, and Davy became famous.

Nitrous oxide is now regarded as dangerous to play with, but dentists still use the gas to relax a nervous patient. It is also used commercially to foam nondairy whipped cream.

A third nitrogen oxide is dinitrogen trioxide (N_2O_3). It exists as a solid only at low temperatures because if it is heated, it instantly decomposes, or breaks up, into NO and NO_2. Dinitrogen tetroxide (N_2O_4) and dinitrogen pentoxide (N_2O_5) readily decompose into the simpler oxides. There may be other oxides of nitrogen.

NO_x names are confusing because their common names are so much alike. During the remainder of this book, the following names will be used to indicate the chemical make-up of the different molecules:

COMPOUNDS THAT MAKE UP NOx

NO – nitrogen monoxide, instead of nitric oxide; "mono" means "one"

NO_2 – nitrogen dioxide; "di" means "two"

N_2O – dinitrogen monoxide, instead of nitrous oxide

Joining a Radical Group

Nitrogen atoms are part of several very important partial molecules called radicals. Also called groups, these partial molecules stay together during a chemical process. The radical called a nitro group, for example, is written as —NO_2. The dash indicates that the radical is usually attached to other atoms. Nitro groups are most often bound to carbon and are important in many organic (carbon-containing) compounds.

The radical called an amide group is made up of a nitrogen atom attached to a carbon atom that is double-bonded to an oxygen atom:

The strong synthetic fiber called nylon is an amide, as is the drug lysergic acid (LSD). Amides are also involved in the digestive process.

A radical called an amine group consists of a nitrogen atom attached to two hydrogen atoms, —NH_2. Amines are important chemicals in our bodies. For example, our nerve cells do not actually touch one another; there is a small gap between them. However, a nerve impulse can jump the gap because the amine called choline carries the impulse across the gap to the next nerve cell.

Amine radicals often form when plant or animal products decay. Such amines smell very bad. Two repellant-smelling amines have similarly repellant names: cadaverine and putrescine.

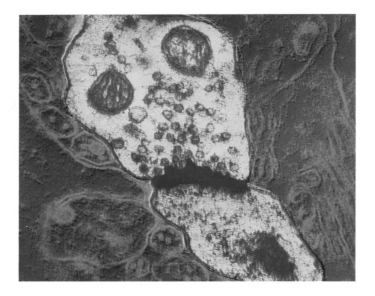

Human nerve cells (shown here dyed blue and green) do not actually touch one another. A nitrogen-containing chemical called choline (colored red and yellow) carries the nerve impulse across the gap between the two nerves.

Nitrogen for Industry

Four of the ten top-selling chemicals produced for industrial use contain nitrogen. Ammonia is first on the list in most countries, and pure nitrogen—both liquid and gas—is fifth. Nitric acid (HNO_3) has become the foundation of the fertilizer industry and also is used in making of dyes and explosives.

Liquid nitrogen is obtained in the process of making liquid oxygen. First, the water vapor and the carbon dioxide are removed from air, usually by cooling it. Then the air is compressed into a very tight space, while it is cooled even further, to almost −200°C (−328°F).

The reduced temperature and the increased pressure change the gas into liquid air. Then the temperature is raised again. Each element in the mixture that makes up air turns back into a gas, or evaporates, at a different temperature. This allows each gas to be drawn off separately. It is then stored in heavy cylinders that keep it compressed as a liquid.

Diatomic nitrogen evaporates at −196°C (−321°F). It leaves behind a mixture of oxygen and argon. Argon evaporates at a temperature just slightly warmer. What remains is nearly pure liquid oxygen.

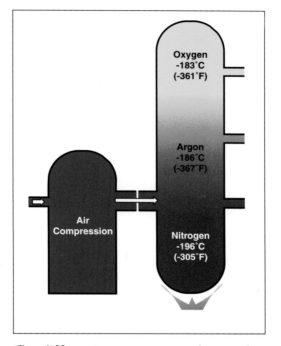

The different components that make up the mixture of cold compressed liquid air evaporate at different temperatures when the liquid air is heated.

IN AND ON THE EARTH

Nitrogen exists naturally in our planet's atmosphere. More than 78 percent of the air we breathe is N_2, the diatomic molecule. It does nothing to us or for us when we breathe it in and it is exhaled unchanged. The nitrogen needed by our bodies can be obtained only by eating plants or animals that ate plants.

In the list of nitrogen compounds on the next page, "clean" and "dry" have to be specified because the parts-per-million measurement changes with the amount of moisture in the air. Also, different locations will have differing amounts of nitrogen compounds in the air because the number of internal-combustion engines that release various nitrogen oxides in exhaust changes from place to place.

The power in a bolt of lightning changes diatomic nitrogen in air into ions that can be used by plants.

NITROGEN COMPOUNDS NEAR EARTH'S SURFACE

Clean, dry air at or near the surface of the planet contains the following nitrogen compounds (in ppm, or parts per million, of air):

diatomic nitrogen (N_2) – 780,900 ppm

ammonia (NH_3) – 0.006 ppm

nitrogen dioxide (NO_2) – 0.006 ppm

dinitrogen monoxide (N_2O) – 0.5 ppm

nitrogen monoxide (NO) – 0.0006 ppm

Nitrogen in the Air

In nature, nitrogen moves from the atmosphere, into living things, and finally back into the atmosphere. Like most things in nature, this "movement" isn't so simple.

Diatomic nitrogen in the air must be changed into electrically charged molecules called ions before plants can use it. Chemists indicate that an atom or a molecule is an ion by showing a plus sign (+) or minus sign (–) after the element's symbol.

The ionization of nitrogen occurs naturally in one of two ways: by the action of nitrifying bacteria or algae and by the effects of lightning in air. The ionization of nitrogen also occurs as a result of the chemical industry making ammonia to use as fertilizer for crops.

Whichever way they are made, the nitrogen ions enter the soil or ocean, where they are absorbed by plants and used to make proteins. Eventually the plants die, and they decompose primarily through the action of different bacteria (called denitrifying bacteria). The bacteria release nitrogen back into the ocean or atmosphere. Animals are brought into the cycle when they eat the plants, but then animals, too, die and decompose.

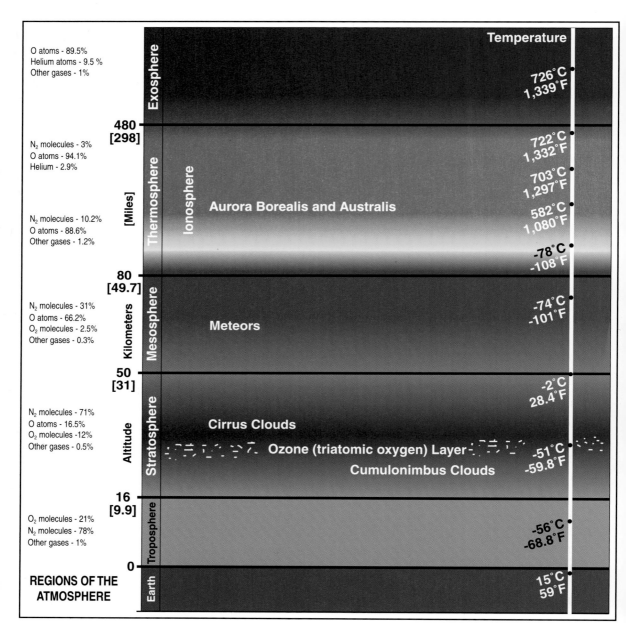

REGIONS OF THE ATMOSPHERE

Temperature

O atoms - 89.5%
Helium atoms - 9.5 %
Other gases - 1%

Exosphere

726°C
1,339°F

480
[298]

N₂ molecules - 3%
O atoms - 94.1%
Helium - 2.9%

Thermosphere

Ionosphere

722°C
1,332°F

703°C
1,297°F

N₂ molecules - 10.2%
O atoms - 88.6%
Other gases - 1.2%

Aurora Borealis and Australis

582°C
1,080°F

-78°C
-108°F

80
[49.7]

N₂ molecules - 31%
O atoms - 66.2%
O₂ molecules - 2.5%
Other gases - 0.3%

Mesosphere

Meteors

-74°C
-101°F

50
[31]

N₂ molecules - 71%
O atoms - 16.5%
O₂ molecules -12%
Other gases - 0.5%

Stratosphere

Cirrus Clouds

Ozone (triatomic oxygen) Layer

Cumulonimbus Clouds

-2°C
28.4°F

-51°C
-59.8°F

16
[9.9]

O₂ molecules - 21%
N₂ molecules - 78%
Other gases - 1%

Troposphere

-56°C
-68.8°F

0

Earth

15°C
59°F

[Miles]

Kilometers

Altitude

Lightning's role in the cycle occurs because the electric discharge raises the temperatures reached by the air molecules as high as 33,000°C (60,000°F). The intense heat makes the N_2 and the O_2 in the atmosphere combine, yielding nitrogen monoxide:

$$N_2 + O_2 \rightarrow 2NO$$

The nitrogen monoxide molecules react with more oxygen to form nitrogen dioxide:

$$2NO + O_2 \rightarrow 2NO_2$$

When water vapor mixes with the nitrogen dioxide, nitric acid and more nitrogen oxide are formed:

$$3NO_2 + H_2O \rightarrow 2HNO_3 + NO$$

The nitric acid falls to the ground, in rain or other precipitation, where it becomes part of the soil. Denitrifying bacteria also produce some N_2O, which rises into the atmosphere.

Into the Atmosphere

The primary nitrogen molecule through the atmosphere is N_2. However, other nitrogen molecules—in tiny quantities—exist at various levels of the atmosphere. Dinitrogen oxide (N_2O) (nitrous oxide) occurs in the troposphere. Above that, in the stratosphere, nitrogen monoxide (NO) occurs. Farther up, in the mesosphere, NO^+ ions can be found all the way out until the atmosphere fades away.

In the stratosphere, at about 21 kilometers (13 mi) up, is a layer of ozone (O_3) that protects earthlings from receiving too much ultraviolet radiation from the sun. Some dinitrogen monoxide (N_2O) rising into the stratosphere reacts with oxygen atoms in that layer to make nitrogen monoxide (NO).

Opposite: A chart of the layers of Earth's atmosphere and the major gases found at the various levels

Instruments aboard satellites reveal the opening, or "hole," in the ozone layer above the Antarctic region.

Some nitrogen monoxide can react with ozone molecules to form an oxygen molecule and nitrogen dioxide. The nitrogen dioxide then reacts with an oxygen atom to form another oxygen molecule, regenerating nitrogen monoxide in the process:

$$O_3 + NO \rightarrow O_2 + NO_2$$

$$NO_2 + O \rightarrow NO + O_2$$

The ozone molecule is gone, but more are regularly made. The energy in solar radiation breaks apart some diatomic oxygen (O_2) molecules, and single O atoms attach themselves to other two-atomed molecules, forming ozone molecules (O_3).

However, humans have affected this process and put it out of balance. For years we've been hearing about the complex manufactured chemicals called CFCs destroying the ozone layer. CFCs are chlorofluorocarbons, compounds of chlorine (Cl, element #17), fluorine (F, #9), and carbon. Jet planes and rockets put additional NO molecules into the stratosphere. Their engines give off NO as exhaust.

Also, in recent years the amount of N_2O in the atmosphere has increased greatly as millions of acres of soil have been exposed when old forests were cut down. Dinitrogen monoxide is one of the results of the decay of biological materials in soil. Normally, it would cycle back into new plants, but if the trees are gone, as they are in much of the tropical rain forests, the dinitrogen monoxide molecules rise into the atmosphere.

Beyond the stratosphere, above 100 kilometers (62 mi), there is still some diatomic nitrogen. When electrically charged particles (especially electrons) making up the solar winds strike the atoms of the gases that exist at that altitude, wonderful swirling colors, called auroras, appear in the sky. They are visible from Earth in the skies toward the north and south poles. The fast-moving electrons strike nitrogen molecules and produce a red color, usually seen as a "fringe" below green wisps produced by electrons colliding with oxygen atoms.

Those same high-altitude nitrogen atoms are bombarded by loose neutrons in cosmic rays from outer space and the sun. When the nucleus of a nitrogen atom takes in a spare neutron, the element itself changes into another element. A common nitrogen atom has a total of 14 neutrons and protons in its nucleus; it is nitrogen-14. When an additional neutron is taken into the nucleus, the number of neutrons becomes 8, but there are still only 7 protons. One proton leaves the nucleus and an electron escapes from the valence shell. The proton and the electron form an atom of a different element—hydrogen. Left behind is an atom with only 6 protons and 6 electrons, but 8 neutrons. What was nitrogen-14 is now carbon-14.

Helping the Nitrogen Cycle

Nitrogen moves through the natural world in what is called the nitrogen cycle. Plants need the element nitrogen to grow. Animals eat plants. The manure, or waste, from animals, as well as the decay of their bodies after death, return nitrogen to the soil, from which plants take it up again.

As we have seen, certain bacteria have the ability to participate in this cycle. They have the ability to change, or "fix," nitrogen in the atmosphere, turning it into a form that plants can absorb. They can change diatomic nitrogen directly into negative ions (atoms with a negative electric charge) called nitrates (NO_3^-). Animals that eat the plants also absorb nitrates, which are remade by animals' bodies into other compounds needed for life.

Humans learned very early that they could help plant crops

When many generations of seabirds nest in one place, their excretions pile up into nitrogen-rich guano.

grow by adding nitrogenous substances, such as animal manure, to the soil. Such an added substance is called fertilizer.

The Indians of Peru knew that the dried excretions of fish-eating birds made good fertilizer. The dried excretions, called *guano*, existed in massive piles on islands off the coast of Peru. Generation after generation of cormorants, penguins, and other birds added to the piles. The foul-smelling powder was rich in nitrogen and phosphate compounds, both of which are needed by crops. (Phosphorus is P, element #15.)

Guano that has hardened into a yellowish mineral is called saltpeter or niter. Such deposits of nitrate minerals are rare because they usually dissolve in water and flow away. Niter deposits are found most often in dry places where little water flows. The largest known deposit is called Chile saltpeter. It is found in a 724-kilometer (450-mi)-long strip in Chile's Atacama Desert. Chile saltpeter is mainly sodium nitrate ($NaNO_3$), but it also contains some potassium nitrate (KNO_3) and other salts.

Before sodium nitrate was found in Chile, Europeans had imported similar potassium nitrate from India, but that supply was nearly exhausted when the South America supply was found.

Sodium nitrate has a somewhat higher percentage of usable nitrogen in it than does potassium nitrate—16 percent, compared to 13 percent. Today, both guano and saltpeter supplies are running out. They have been replaced by synthetic fertilizers.

NITROGEN IN LIVING THINGS

Nitrogen is an essential nutrient for humans and other animals. But our bodies cannot use the element directly. We have to eat plants, which can use nitrogen directly, to get the nitrogen we need. All living animals depend directly or indirectly on plants.

The Nitrogen Fixers

Neither plants nor animals can directly utilize the N_2 gas that exists in the air. Living things use only nitrogen ions. Nitrogen must be changed into ammonium ions (NH_4^+) or nitrate ions (NO_3^-), before our bodies can use it as the nutrient that our bodies need. This process is called "fixing."

An agricultural scientist checks experimental rice fields for the intake of nutrients.

Since life began, and certainly before humans learned about synthetic fertilizers, nitrogen has been fixed by lightning or by the action of certain bacteria. However, many parts of our planet rarely get storms, so bacteria have long been the most important fixers.

Colonies of certain bacteria are found in the roots of various plants, especially legumes, such as peas, beans, and clover. These bacteria have the ability to fix nitrogen. Traditionally, farmers planted legumes in a field one year, plowing them under to let the soil take on lots of nitrogen. Then, the following year, they planted a crop that takes up the nitrogen. Now, however, most farmers in developed countries want to use their fields every year for the same nitrogen-using crops, such as corn. Farmers therefore have to use chemical fertilizers that add nitrogen to the soil. A corn crop contains 41 kilograms (90 lbs) of nitrogen per acre.

Microscopic creatures that have the ability to fix nitrogen are called diazotrophs. Though most diazotrophs are bacteria found in legumes, there are also primitive blue-green algae, called cyanobacteria, that can fix nitrogen. These algae grow in rice paddies, where they attach themselves to a species of water fern. When rice farmers plant this fern in their paddies, nitrogen compounds are fixed and released into the water where they are absorbed by the rice roots.

A Beneficial Infection

Different bacteria carry out different processes as part of the whole nitrogen cycle. Some bacteria called *Nitrosomonas* are nitrifying bacteria. They turn ammonia fertilizer into nitrite ions (NO_2^-). Another group, called *Nitrobacter*, turn NO_2^- ions into nitrate ions (NO_3^-). Still another type of bacteria, denitrifying bacteria, reverses the process, turning NO_3^- and NO_2^- into N_2 and N_2O. The bacteria benefit by getting food from plant tissues, and

Rhizobium bacteria form nodules on the roots of legume plants.
In the nodules, these bacteria fix nitrogen fertilizer into usable
ammonium ions.

the plants get the nitrogen compounds the bacteria produce as
their waste products. Such a relationship is called symbiotic—
both the bacteria and the plants benefit.

Rhizobium is one of the main nitrifying bacteria in legume
roots. It spends part of its life cycle living freely in the soil. Its
protective coat, called the capsule, keeps it from drying out as
the soil dries. Later, when Rhizobium moves into the roots of a
legume, the sticky capsule helps it cling to the root hairs. In
many legumes, especially clovers, peanuts, and soybeans, col-
lections of the bacteria form a nodule, or small lump, on the
root, in which they carry on their nitrogen-fixing process. The
plant could be said to be "infected" with the bacterium, but this
is definitely a beneficial infection.

Nitrogen-fixing bacteria contain a special enzyme called nitrogenase. This enzyme, which may be likened to a biological
catalyst, has the ability to change the nitrogen molecule in air

(N$_2$) into NH$_3$, or ammonia. Nitrogenase contains sulfur (S, element #16) and iron (Fe, #26), as well as the element molybdenum (Mo, #42), which is not usually a part of living organisms. The structure of nitrogenase was not discovered until 1992.

Nitrogen Fertilizers

Nitrogen is taken into plants either because of the action of nitrogen-fixing bacteria or because a farmer applies ammonia-based fertilizers to his fields. The nitrogen in fertilizer can exist in several different ways. It can be variations of ammonium, such as ammonium sulfate, ammonium nitrate, or ammonium phosphate. It can also be in a nitrate, such as calcium nitrate or ammonium nitrate. Or it may exist as a compound called urea, which breaks down into ammonium salts.

Most farmers in the United States use chemical fertilizers based on ammonia, which is 82 percent nitrogen. These are called inorganic fertilizers.

Farmers who use organic rather than synthetic fertilizers may use bloodmeal, manure, or sludge. Bloodmeal is a powdered dried blood that contains 15 percent nitrogen. Manure was the original source of organic fertilizer, but it is not a really concentrated source of nitrogen. Even the sludge from sewage-treatment plants contains only about 2 percent nitrogen. Wet sludge, however, can be concentrated and dried, which increases the nitrogen content to almost 6 percent.

Magical Building Blocks

To get the nitrogen we need, we can eat plants, or we can eat animals that have eaten plants, or we can eat both. Regardless of how we get the NH$_3$ group, our bodies utilize it in many different ways.

Remember the amine group described earlier? It is NH$_3$ with two hydrogen atoms and the nitrogen attached to a carbon atom.

Two biochemists studying a model of a protein molecule. Proteins are among the most complex molecules known.

If an amine is attached to a carbon atom that is then bonded to a COOH group (which is called a carboxyl group), the result is an amino acid. Amino acids are the building blocks of protein, the main constituent of all living things. As proteins are broken down, the energy given off is used to maintain life processes. Twenty amino acids are vital to humans. Some of them are essential amino acids and come from the food we eat. Others are called nonessential because they can be produced by the body from other amino acids or other organic chemicals in the body. We do not need to get them from food.

It takes many amino acid groups fastened together to make one of the body's complex protein molecules. All proteins include at least twelve groups. When the proteins are eaten, digestion breaks them down again into different amino acids that are put together in other ways to build up new proteins.

For example, carnitine is a protein needed by the body to oxidize complex fatty acids, the main compounds in fats.

Carnitine is manufactured in the liver and kidneys out of two amino acids called glutamine and methionine. It is also present in the meat and dairy products we eat. Hair and fingernails are made up of another protein called keratin, and cartilage, tendons, and bone are made up of a protein called collagen. Collagen from cattle is used to make gelatine.

Animal proteins are generally complete—they include all the essential amino acids we need. Plant proteins are less complete, but they come in such variety that, with a little planning, vegetarians can get the protein they need for a healthy diet although they never eat meat.

Removing Nitrogen

Animals take in more nitrogen from the food they eat than their bodies can use, even though about 16 percent of the protein molecules in the body require nitrogen. When protein breaks down, much of it turns into ammonia, which has to be eliminated, or excreted.

Most fish give off ammonia itself. During respiration, ammonia flows out across their gills as oxygen flows in. The bodies of mammals—and some other animals, including sharks—don't have such a convenient arrangement. To prevent the build-up of ammonia in the blood, other ways are used to get rid of it.

In humans, as the blood carrying ammonia moves through the liver, the ammonia is changed into the chemical urea, $CO(NH_2)_2$, also known as carbamide. In the kidneys, the urea is turned into part—up to 5 percent—of urine and excreted. If there isn't enough water circulating through and out of the body to keep the kidneys functioning properly, ammonia quickly builds up and becomes toxic.

Urea was the first organic chemical ever produced in the laboratory. When Friedrich Wöhler, a German chemist, first produced urea in 1828, other chemists reluctantly had to give up the

Synthetic urea that has been melted and recrystallized takes on an array of beautiful colors.

belief that only a "vital force" that exists in living things could produce such organic, or carbon-containing, chemicals.

More than 100 years later, Hans Adolf Krebs, another German chemist, studied urea again. He showed that in order for amino acids to be broken down for their energy, the nitrogen atoms must be removed. When the amino group in an amino acid breaks off and reacts with ammonia, it forms the complex urea molecule.

Synthetic urea is used as a fertilizer and is produced by uniting liquid ammonia and liquid carbon dioxide. At high temperatures and under high pressure, these two chemicals combine to make ammonium carbamate, which readily decomposes into urea and water.

The process also happens in reverse. Urea used as a fertilizer is distributed in soil as a crystal or powder. When water is added, through irrigation or rain, the urea changes back into ammonium carbamate and then into ammonia and carbon dioxide. Both these chemicals can be used as nutrients by plant crops. Synthetic urea can also be combined with a chemical called formaldehyde to form a base for a variety of plastics.

Plants and Animals—Close Relatives

Hemoglobin is the compound in blood that takes oxygen from the lungs and carries it to the cells. Central to this compound is a ring-shaped molecule called porphyrin. This molecule is a complex structure made up on a base of four nitrogen atoms. The porphyrin ring combines with an atom of iron and then attaches itself to a protein molecule, making hemoglobin. The nonprotein part of the molecule is called heme.

In 1997, a paleontologist hunting for fossils and other signs of ancient living things, discovered for the first time some heme remaining in a dinosaur fossil.

A similar porphyrin molecule combines with magnesium (Mg, element #12) to make chlorophyll—the green matter in plants. Chlorophyll has the ability, in the presence of sunlight, to turn carbon dioxide and water into food.

When hemoglobin breaks down after about twenty days of circulating through the body in blood, the heme portions of the molecules collect. They create the yellow and brown colors of our bodies' excretions. After the heme portions have separated, the substances that remain still contain almost 150 amino acid groups. These groups then reorganize themselves into other proteins that are utilized by the body.

AMMONIA: TODAY'S VITAL CHEMICAL

When nitrogen is fixed by bacteria, the main product is ammonia, NH_3. Ammonia got its name in ancient times when it was made from nitrogenous waste by priests at the Egyptian temple dedicated to the god Ammon.

Ammonia is a pungent (sharp-smelling), colorless gas at room temperature. When cooled to $-33.35°C$ ($-28.3°F$) and compressed, it becomes liquid. Liquid ammonia can easily be carried in railway tank cars or tanker trucks. If the pressure is released, the liquid changes back into a gas, absorbing a great deal of heat in the process. This trait has made ammonia useful as a cooling liquid in large

The legs holding up the TransAlaska oil pipeline are kept cold with refrigeration by ammonia.

industrial refrigeration systems. If the metal legs holding up the TransAlaska oil pipeline weren't chilled, the permanently frozen ground on which the pipeline was built would melt from the heat caused by the oil flowing through the pipe. Ammonia is the refrigerating gas that keeps the supporting pipeline legs cool.

The Ammonia Makers

Knowing how useful natural nitrogen sources are, chemists sought ways to produce ammonia in the laboratory. The first person to collect ammonia gas (NH_3) was English chemist Joseph Priestley in 1774. The actual composition of ammonia (nitrogen and hydrogen) was identified ten years later by a French scientist, Claude Berthollet.

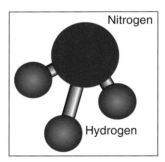

NH_3, the ammonia molecule

In later years, ammonia was produced in fairly small amounts by separating nitrogen from liquefied air. That nitrogen was heated with calcium carbide (CaC_2) to make calcium cyanamide (CaNCN). Ammonia was then produced by treating the calcium cyanamide with steam under pressure. The hydrogen in the water molecules of the steam linked up with the nitrogen atoms in the calcium cyanamide making ammonia.

About 1908, a German chemist, Fritz Haber, became the first person to finally make ammonia directly from the nitrogen in air. In what has come to be called the Haber Process, he made a gaseous mixture of three parts hydrogen and one part nitrogen. He compressed the mixture and then passed it over hot iron (Fe, element #26) filings. The iron filings were a catalyst—they served only to speed up the process but were not used up. The chemical equation for this process is:

$$N_2 + 3H_2 \rightarrow 2NH_3$$

The central task of an ammonia manufacturing plant (above) is to make ammonia by the Haber-Bosch Process seen below.

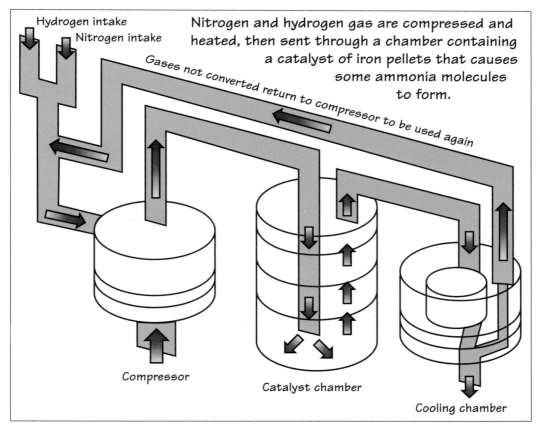

Hydrogen intake

Nitrogen intake

Nitrogen and hydrogen gas are compressed and heated, then sent through a chamber containing a catalyst of iron pellets that causes some ammonia molecules to form.

Gases not converted return to compressor to be used again

Compressor

Catalyst chamber

Cooling chamber

During World War I, the Germans used Haber's powerful, corrosive ammonia gas as a source of nitrogen chemicals to produce explosives. Haber's invention proved useful to the rest of the world, too, and he won the 1918 Nobel Prize in Chemistry for his work. What he didn't win was continuous German approval. Because he was Jewish, he was later forced by Adolf Hitler's persecution of Jews to leave Germany.

Another German chemist, Carl Bosch, adapted the Haber Process for making ammonia in commercial quantities. The ammonia made by the Haber-Bosch Process can be converted to nitric acid (HNO_3) for use in explosives, but even more importantly, it became the basis for producing synthetic fertilizer.

The Ammonium Ion

Ammonia can be used as a fertilizer because it changes into ammonium ions (NH_4^+) when it is mixed with water. These ammonium ions are positive, so they are attracted to soil particles, which have a negative charge. From the soil, the ions can be absorbed by plant roots.

The other form in which plants can take in nitrogen is as a nitrate ion (NO_3^-). But because it is negative, it is not held by the negative soil particles. Nitrate ions are easily washed away.

Oddly enough, ammonia (NH_3), is a base, the chemical opposite of an acid. This is odd because bases usually contain a hydroxide ion (OH^-). By definition, a base is a substance that takes on a proton, which is the equivalent of a hydrogen ion (H^+). A hydroxide ion—from a base—that takes on a hydrogen ion—from an acid—forms neutral water.

But ammonia is different. It takes a proton from water, becoming an ammonium ion and a hydroxide ion:

$$NH_3 + H_2O \rightarrow NH_4^+ + OH^-$$

Actually, most of the ions formed react readily with each

other, turning back into ammonia and water. Only a few remain as ammonium and hydroxide ions, so ammonia is referred to as a weak base. Ammonium itself does not have an odor, but it readily decomposes into ammonia, which has the odor that is familiar to anyone who has changed a baby's diapers.

Feeding the World

Because of its ability to turn into nutrients needed for crops to grow, ammonia has become one of the most important gases produced by the chemical industry. The gas can be injected

Dry ammonium nitrate being applied to a field by a spreader. Rain or irrigation water carries the fertilizer into the soil and converts the compound into ammonium ions.

Ammonia: Today's Vital Chemical

directly into the soil from tanks wheeled into the fields. However, it is more often combined with nitric acid to produce ammonium nitrate. This white powder spread on the soil reacts with water to form ions.

Liquid ammonia can be injected into the ground, several inches below the surface where it can't evaporate. Ammonia also may be added directly to irrigation water or applied as dry pellets that release their nitrogen content when the soil is watered.

Other Uses

Ammonia is also a source of hydrogen gas for industry. It's safer to transport liquid ammonia than hydrogen, which can explode. After ammonia reaches its destination, it is heated slightly to make it decompose into nitrogen and hydrogen.

Ammonia easily dissolves in water, making a chemical called ammonium hydroxide, or ammonia water. One part water will dissolve 400 parts ammonia. A 28 percent solution of ammonia water is used as a cleaning agent to dissolve grease on windows and other surfaces.

The first ammonia made commercially for cleaning was cloudy. The Haber Process produced ammonia that was clear, but the public rejected it. People thought the chemical had to be cloudy to work well in cleaning. So manufacturers made it cloudy again—by adding soap to the liquid.

In the late nineteenth century, fashion required women to wear corsets so tight that the women could barely breathe. With too little oxygen reaching their hearts, they often fainted—which became a fashionable thing to do. To help them regain consciousness after fainting, they carried pretty bottles of "smelling salts" that gave off a strong, piercing odor. The smelling salts consisted of perfumed ammonium carbonate. Breathing the gas given off by the crystals caused the person inhaling it to take sharp breaths that quickly revived them.

NITROGEN COMPOUNDS THAT POLLUTE

Nitrogen plays a positive role in our lives. Unfortunately, it also plays a negative role in making our planet a less pleasant place to live. There are a number of environmental dangers—to air and water and human life—that are caused by compounds containing nitrogen.

Engines and NO_x

Automobiles and trucks contribute about 14 percent of the chemicals that pollute our air. The main pollutants are the various nitrogen oxides (NO_x) given off automatically by internal combustion engines. Air is taken into the engine where the oxygen in it makes the fuel burn. However, not all the air is used

The air in a city is often polluted by compounds given off in the exhaust of automobile engines.

39

in the combustion reaction. Some air passes back out, but not before the heat causes the N_2 and O_2 in the air to change into nitrogen monoxide:

$$N_2 + O_2 + heat \rightarrow 2NO$$

As soon as the NO has formed, some of it reacts with the oxygen in the air to form nitrogen dioxide, which is a major part of the air pollution called smog:

$$2NO + O_2 \rightarrow 2NO_2$$

The state of California led the way in demanding that automobile engines meet certain standards in preventing pollution. Before 1966, for every mile driven, cars gave off 10.6 grams (0.371 oz) of hydrocarbons, 84 grams (2.94 oz) of carbon dioxide, and 4.1 g (0.14 oz) of nitrogen oxides.

More efficient engines helped reduce pollution, but the main thing that eased automotive pollution was the installation of

A cutaway view of a catalytic converter that mounts under a car

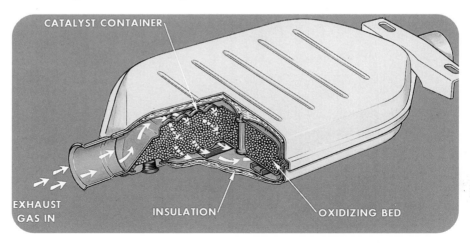

CATALYST CONTAINER

EXHAUST GAS IN

INSULATION

OXIDIZING BED

devices called catalytic converters. A catalytic converter is a device with such precious metals as platinum (Pt, element #78) on many of its surfaces. These metals are catalysts, which gives the device the name "catalytic converter."

Pollutants such as nitrogen oxides are adsorbed by the metallic surfaces. That's not the same as *ab*sorbed, in which a substance is taken into another. An *ad*sorbed substance attaches itself to the surface of something. In a catalytic converter, the NO molecules break apart, leaving N and O atoms free to wander the platinum-coated metallic surfaces. If two N atoms chance to meet, they form N_2, which floats off (desorbs) from the surface into the air. Similarly, O atoms form O_2 and desorb. The diatomic nitrogen and oxygen molecules are harmless.

Other compounds left by engine combustion also are affected by the catalytic converter. Hydrocarbons (HC compounds) and carbon monoxide (CO) are turned into less harmful carbon dioxide (CO_2) and water.

The catalytic converter program has worked well in reducing pollutants. In 1993, the limits set by California almost thirty years before were met. Today, cars in proper running order give off only 0.25 gram (0.009 oz) of hydrocarbons, 3.4 grams (0.119 oz) of carbon dioxide, and 0.4 gram (0.014 oz) of nitrogen oxides.

Continuing to React

Nevertheless, some nitrogen pollutants from car engines are left even after passing through an efficient catalytic converter. Although the damage they do is less now than it was twenty years ago, such pollutants can still react with the natural gases in the air to turn into harmful chemicals.

Brown haze in smog comes from the presence of nitrogen dioxide, NO_2, a reddish-brown gas formed when nitrogen monoxide, NO, is formed. This happens especially on hot, windless days when there's lots of traffic. In the presence of sunlight,

When the needles of conifer trees are damaged by acid rain, the entire structure and functioning of the trees can be harmed.

the NO_2 separates into nitrogen monoxide (NO), and an oxygen atom. That loose oxygen atom then quickly joins a diatomic oxygen molecule to make ozone, O_3. Ozone damages lungs, destroys plant tissues, and even harms automobile tires.

When NO_2 enters the air, it can undergo various reactions. Depending on local conditions, some of those reactions lead to the formation of nitric acid, or HNO_3. This acid can be carried to the ground with rain in what has come to be called acid rain. If the acid rain lands on soil, there is no harm done. It just contributes to the nitrogen in soil. But if it lands on towns and cities, it can cause damage. Airborne nitric acid has been known to eat through car paint and make holes in clothing hanging on a line. In addition, nitric acid can be carried by the wind from cities where it was formed to the countryside, where it can do major harm to crops and forests.

Many scientists think our planet is getting warmer. This "global warming" is usually blamed on an increase in carbon dioxide (CO_2) in the atmosphere from cars and coal-burning power plants and from burning down tropical rain forests. However, dinitrogen oxide (N_2O) is 200 to 300 times more effective than carbon dioxide in holding heat in our atmosphere.

Individual molecules of N_2O also last up to twenty times longer in the atmosphere than CO_2 molecules do—perhaps as long as 150 years. Not until the N_2O molecules have risen high into the stratosphere—17 to 48 kilometers (11 to 30 mi) above Earth's surface—are they broken by sunlight into their original diatomic nitrogen and oxygen. We can never eliminate all the N_2O because it is made by natural processes in the soil, not just by human activity.

Awash in Nitrogen

Nitrogen compounds don't pollute only the air. Even though such compounds are needed by plants, trouble begins if more nitrogen compounds are added to the soil than can be taken up by plants.

Nitrogen fertilizers change into nitrate ions. Rain or irrigation water can wash, or leach, excess nitrate ions into the shallow groundwater supply. Drinking water containing nitrates is harmful to the human digestive system. Bacteria that are normally found within the body can turn the nitrates (NO_3^-) into nitrites (NO_2^-). Nitrites can attach themselves to the hemoglobin molecules in our blood. When that happens, there is no place on the molecules for diatomic oxygen molecules from the lungs to attach themselves. So insufficient oxygen reaches the cells.

Infants are most at risk from nitrates in drinking water because older children and adults have enough acidity in their stomachs to kill the bacteria that change nitrates into nitrites. But babies who don't get enough oxygen can develop a sometimes fatal disease called methemoglobinemia, or "blue-baby syndrome." If a family's water supply gets nitrates in it, a tiny baby should be fed breast milk or a formula that does not have to be mixed with water.

The maximum level of nitrates in well water considered safe is only 10 parts per million (ppm) for infants and 45 ppm for adults. If a private well is found to contain nitrates, the water can be treated before it is used for drinking and cooking. This can be done with a device that exchanges negative nitrate ions for ions that are less harmful. (This device is similar to a water softener that exchanges positive ions.)

It would be too costly to treat the water for an entire city with an ion-exchange device, however. Instead, a municipal water-treatment plant will often put part of the water through an ion-exchange system and then mix it back into the regular water supply. This process dilutes the nitrates in the water.

Some major cities have dug huge reservoirs where the water is allowed to sit for a long period. Nitrates gradually disappear from sitting water by reacting with the oxygen in the air. Just before use, chlorine (Cl, element #17) is added to the reservoir's water to kill bacteria.

What to Do

Obviously, many of our planet's environmental problems arise because of the amount of nitrogen fertilizer used by the world's farmers. There are steps farmers can take to prevent nitrate build-up in the soil. They can:

• use only as much fertilizer as is actually needed to produce a healthy crop;

• not depend on chemical fertilizer for all the nitrogen needs of the crop; there are many other sources of nitrogen, such as legume crops;

• apply fertilizer immediately before the main growth period so that it doesn't lie in the soil long before being taken up;

• use manures as much as possible. Their nitrates do not leach as deeply into the soil as those from artificial fertilizers;

• have the soil tested in June (after the soil has warmed up) for the presence of nitrates rather than automatically fertilizing every growing season.

EXPLOSIVE EPISODES

An explosion can occur when a substance changes from a liquid or a solid to a gas very quickly. When the nitrogen in nitrogen compounds is released rapidly as gas, a great deal of heat energy is given off. This kind of reaction makes nitrogen the main chemical in many explosives.

Gunpowder

Gunpowder was used in ancient times in China and India. In Europe, the ingredients of gunpowder were described by English philosopher-chemist Roger Bacon in a letter written in 1247. He said that gunpowder was a mixture of about 75 percent saltpeter, 15 percent charcoal, and 10 percent sulfur. Because of that letter, Roger Bacon has been credited with discovering gunpowder. However, newer research indicates that gunpowder was already being used in Germany.

Fireworks are one of the oldest known uses of gunpowder, the original nitrogen explosive.

Old-time gunpowder gave off dense black smoke when it was ignited. Anyone using it became completely covered in black soot. In wartime, the entire scene of battle could gradually disappear from sight as the sky became dark with soot.

Starting about 1630, a new use was found for the so-called black powder. It began to be used to break up rock in mines. However, its use was limited by the difficulty in obtaining saltpeter, which at that time had to come from India.

The United States has some saltpeter, in the form of calcium nitrate [$Ca(NO_3)_2$] found in dry, sheltered limestone caves where bats have lived. In the early history of the nation, saltpeter was obtained from caves in the Appalachian Mountains. During the Civil War, saltpeter for making powder to use in firearms was obtained from Kentucky's Mammoth Cave.

Beyond Black Powder

Enter Christian Schönbein in the 1840s, a German chemist who had earlier discovered ozone (O_3). To his wife's dismay, Schönbein was experimenting in her kitchen when he found that nitric acid applied to cotton (that same dismayed wife's apron) became highly flammable. He had made a chemical he called guncotton, or nitrocellulose. It was smokeless, making it better than gunpowder. German explosives manufacturers enthusiastically took to guncotton—until too many factories exploded because of the chemical's instability. Nitrocellulose is still used to a small extent in submarine torpedoes because it will explode when wet. It also is used to propel small-arms ammunition.

Today, guncotton is called cellulose nitrate. The chemical has many uses, depending on the amount of nitrogen in it. Both printing inks and rocket propellants, for example, contain cellulose nitrate, but the ink contains less nitrogen than the fuel. Cellulose nitrate mixed with an oily varnish is used to coat leather, making patent leather.

The remains of mining equipment used to obtain saltpeter from Mammoth Cave during the U.S. Civil War

Also during the 1840s, Ascanio Sobrero, a professor at the University of Turin in Italy, mixed nitrogen and sulfuric acid into glycerin, which is a thick liquid alcohol usually derived from the process of making soaps. Pure glycerin is called glycerol, with the formula $C_3H_5(OH)_3$. Today, glycerin is usually obtained from petroleum.

Sobrero's discovery was glyceryl trinitrate, better known as nitroglycerin. It is a yellow oil that is very unstable because it contains within its complex molecule both an oxidizer and a fuel that can explode. Every molecule is packed with its own explosive.

Nitroglycerin has a quite different use in medicine. When diluted and absorbed by the body, it causes the muscles controlling the diameter of arteries to expand. The blood flows more easily through the blood vessels, and the person's blood pressure goes down. This eases the work the heart must do to keep pumping.

For emergency home use, nitroglycerin comes as a small, quickly dissolving tablet placed under the tongue (where blood vessels are nearest to the surface). It can also be a liquid that is absorbed continuously from a skin patch.

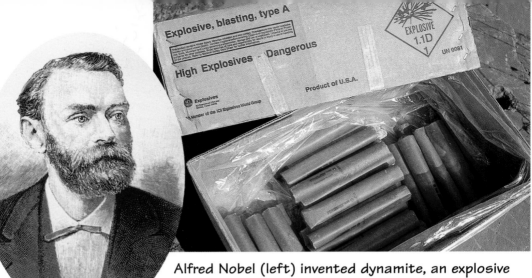

Alfred Nobel (left) invented dynamite, an explosive that can be handled safely in sticks because it can be set off only by a detonator.

Making It Safer

Swedish industrialist Alfred Nobel became convinced that a safe way to handle glyceryl trinitrate had to be found after his brother was killed in an explosion in Nobel's own factory. In 1866, Nobel made nitroglycerin stable by converting it to a solid that he called dynamite, which could be packed in paper cylinders. Nobel's dynamite is a mixture of 75 percent nitroglycerin and 25 percent diatomaceous earth. Diatomaceous earth is a chalky material found in ancient deposits of the shells of microscopic algae called diatoms. Dynamite requires a small explosion by a detonator, or blasting cap, to set it off.

Alfred Nobel hated to see his invention used in war. He wanted it used for such purposes as opening the American West to railroads and making the work of miners less backbreaking. Since he had no control over his invention's use, he left his fortune to the founding of prizes to be awarded annually for achievements in peace, sciences, and literature.

In 1889, Sir Frederick Abel of England mixed nitrocellulose with nitroglycerin and added some petroleum jelly. This procedure stabilized the explosive material and allowed it to be formed into soft cords, that could be placed around objects that were to be blown up. Abel gave his invention the name *cordite*.

TNT is trinitrotoluene, a high explosive discovered by German scientist J. Wilbrand in 1863. It was not used until just before World War I, when a cheap way was found to get toluene to react with nitric acid in the presence of a sulfuric acid catalyst. The result is a colorless crystal in the shape of thin icicles.

TNT is safer to handle than nitroglycerin because it will burn without exploding. TNT melts at a fairly low temperature (81°C; 178°F), and liquid TNT can be poured into shells or land mines for use in weapons. It will not even explode when the weapon is fired. Only when the smaller explosion of a detonator is set off first will the TNT explode.

A related explosive called RDX is blended with plastic to make a material that can be molded. It is used most frequently in demolishing steel-reinforced concrete buildings.

Ammonium Nitrate

Before World War I, German chemists discovered that they could make explosive ammonium nitrate by combining ammonia with nitric acid:

$$HNO_3 + NH_3 \rightarrow NH_4NO_3.$$

Germany was initially interested in the crystalline solid's potential as an explosive, but the chemical later turned out to be useful as a fertilizer. Unfortunately, the useful and the harmful often go together.

On April 16, 1947, a French ship, the *Grandcamp,* was floating in the harbor at Texas City, Texas, loaded with ammonium nitrate fertilizer. A small fire in the hold of the ship was thought to be extinguished, but restarted itself. The ship exploded, setting off another blast at a nearby Monsanto Chemical plant. That

The remains of the federal building in Oklahoma City, Oklahoma, seen at night after a bomb containing ammonium nitrate was exploded there

blast, in turn, ignited fires at several oil refineries. In addition, another ship loaded with ammonium nitrate exploded hours later. It took three days for all the fires to be put out.

In this largest industrial accident in American history, 552 people were killed, including some people 3.2 kilometers (2 mi) away. An additional 2,000 residents of the 15,000-person city were injured. Windows were blown out of buildings 18 kilometers (11 mi) across the bay in Galveston.

That blast was an accident, but in 1995, ammonium nitrate was used deliberately to blow up the federal building in Oklahoma City, Oklahoma. Found guilty of the deed was Timothy McVeigh, an antigovernment activist. He had rented a truck and filled it with 907 kilograms (2,000 lbs) of ammonium nitrate fertilizer. He moved the truck adjacent to the federal building, ignited racing-car fuel as a detonator, and then walked away. The ammonium nitrate exploded, killing 168 people, including 19 children in a day-care center. This was the most deadly terrorist attack in U.S. history.

Today, chemists are at work to find a practical way to remove the explosive qualities of agricultural-grade ammonium nitrate. Some nations require that it be sold only when diluted with a nonexploding and nonnutritive material such as limestone.

A NITROGEN CATALOG

Recycling in a Fish Tank

One of the main perils of being a fish in an aquarium is the build-up of nitrogen in the closed system. The fishes' nitrogenous wastes quickly convert to ammonia. If ammonia is allowed to accumulate for even a few hours, it quickly reaches a toxic level. The aquarium keeper must make certain that the ammonia is converted to less harmful nitrogen compounds. Once again, nitrogen-converting bacteria are the answer.

Traditionally, bacteria were allowed to accumulate on the gravel in the bottom of a fish tank. But now most tank owners use biological filters to encourage bacterial growth. These filters contain a foam cartridge or numerous foam blocks that have a huge amount of

A foam cartridge for a fish-tank filter has millions of tiny holes in which denitrifying bacteria can grow.

surface on which bacteria grow. The tank's pump forces water to flow continuously across the bacterial surface.

Such bacteria aren't something you have to buy—they exist in the air and will settle into the tank when ammonia is present. The nitrite-forming bacteria will settle first, then the nitrate-forming bacteria will collect.

Nitrites can also build up in a fish tank, which is why tanks need regular partial changes of the water. Without such changes, the nitrites can damage your fishes' nervous system, liver, and kidneys.

Silver Nitrate in Photography

Thomas Wedgwood, the son of a great ceramics designer in England, made the first steps in photography. In the late 1700s, he figured out that he could make an image on glass of a painting by letting sunlight reflected from the picture strike a coating of silver nitrate ($AgNO_3$), applied to a glass plate. (Silver is Ag, element #47.) The coating turned various shades of gray and black in response to the reflected light.

It was several decades before Louis Daguerre of France made photography practical. He used silver iodide, AgI, which is more sensitive than silver nitrate, to coat a glass plate on which an image could be made by sunlight. (Iodine is I, element #53.)

Today, silver nitrate is used once more in the emulsion—the coating applied to the film. When the film is being manufactured, silver nitrate reacts with potassium bromide to produce silver bromide and potassium nitrate. (Bromine is Br, element #35.) The potassium nitrate is washed away, and the film you buy for your camera is coated only with silver bromide.

Early versions of film itself were made from cellulose nitrate, but that material was highly flammable. Many photographers were burned when their film caught fire. Today, cellulose nitrate film has been replaced by so-called safety film.

A diver explores deep in the ocean, using scuba gear to breathe.

Diving into the Bends

People who dive deep in the ocean use tanks of compressed air to breathe. If they dive too deep and come back to the surface too fast, they are susceptible to a painful condition known as decompression sickness, or the bends.

As a diver goes deeper in the water, the pressure from the weight of the water increases. The amount of nitrogen dissolved in body tissues, especially fat, also increases. When the diver heads back toward the surface, the pressure decreases and nitrogen bubbles out of the tissues unless the ascent is taken very slowly. If a fast ascent is necessary in an emergency, the nitrogen bubbles can block the flow of blood and enter joints, causing intense pain. To prevent the bends, a diver must ascend at a specified rate. Also, divers can have their compressed-air tanks filled with a mixture of oxygen and helium (He, element #2) instead of nitrogen. Helium does not cause the bends.

Decompression sickness can be relieved by putting the person in a decompression chamber, which is slowly brought back to the normal pressure of 1 atmosphere (1,013 millibars; 14.6 pounds per square inch). If necessary, the diver can be sent into the depths again to ascend slowly.

Making Light

The common battery used in flashlights contains zinc chloride ($ZnCl_2$) and ammonium chloride (NH_4Cl) in a paste. The paste lies between a negatively charged metal called the anode (actually the metal case) and a positively charged metal called the cathode. The carbon rod that goes through the middle of the paste is the cathode. When the battery is connected in a circuit, the NH_4Cl ionizes, releasing electrons. The electrons flow as electricity from the anode, through the lightbulb, to the cathode.

Nitrogen also plays a role in the lightbulbs themselves. Ordinary incandescent lightbulbs, for example, are filled with nitrogen gas. The thin filaments that glow in a bulb last longer when the bulb is filled with nitrogen instead of oxygen. The use of nitrogen instead of oxygen also slows the process of tiny fragments of filament breaking off. These fragments blacken the inside of the bulb.

Saving Lives

Air bags are installed in cars to prevent people in the front seat from going through the windshield during an accident. The bags have long been rapidly inflated by an explosive reaction

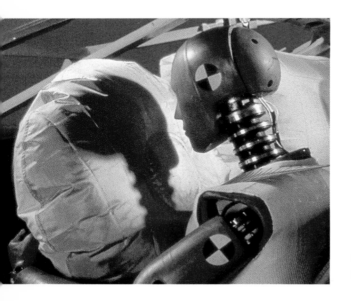

(contained within a canister) that instantly produces nitrogen gas. However, the explosive chemical used is both corrosive and toxic.

Manufacturers are investigating new chemicals that will expand the air bag just as rapidly but without the corrosion and toxicity. Although one method involves the expansion of argon,

A dummy strikes an air bag during a test crash of a car.

most use a nitrogen compound such as ammonium nitrate as the starting point.

Nitrogen has long played another role in automobile safety. The first safety glass, invented in 1910, was made from two thin layers of glass with cellulose nitrate between them.

The Human Silkworm

Rayon, originally called artificial silk, was first produced as early as 1884, by French scientist Comte Hilaire de Chardonnet. The woven material was made of thin strands spun from a solution of cellulose nitrate mixed with ether and alcohol. However, this early version of rayon was highly flammable. Rayon was not made safer until Chardonnet figured out how to remove a nitro group ($—NO_2$) from the material after it was spun by using a special chemical solvent. Today, nitrogen is involved in the production of many synthetic fabrics, though cellulose nitrate has been replaced by cellulose acetate, which is produced from acetic acid instead of nitric acid.

The Lone Nitro

Compounds containing the nitro group ($—NO_2$) are exceedingly rare in living organisms. The first one found was located in a mold, which produced an antibiotic used to fight disease. Its chemical name of chloramphenicol does not even acknowledge that there is a nitro group in it. Although it is not used a great deal today, chloramphenicol was extremely useful in the treatment of typhoid fever and whooping cough.

Nice Nitric Acid

Some people complain regularly that they have headaches or perpetual colds because of "sinus trouble." The sinuses are spaces, or cavities, in the skull, especially around the nose and in the forehead. Sinuses probably keep the skull from being too heavy. That's a good thing, but in some people the sinuses also regularly become infected by bacteria.

The odd thing is that most people don't get such infections. Their sinuses stay clear of bacteria. Scientists at the Karolinska Institute in Sweden have discovered that the sinuses of people who don't get infections are lined with cells that produce large quantities of nitrogen monoxide (NO), which prevents bacteria from multiplying.

Quick Freezing

Liquid nitrogen is the chemical of choice used in flash-freezing food. The food moves on a factory conveyor belt through a chamber where it is sprayed with liquid nitrogen. The food freezes almost instantly—so quickly that the ice crystals that normally form in freezing food are almost nonexistent. This method is particularly useful for foods that turn mushy when ice crystals in them melt.

The Color Purple, and Others

In 1856, 18-year-old British chemistry student William Henry Perkin, was experimenting with aniline. This molecule consists of a benzene ring (six carbon atoms arranged in a circle, each with a hydrogen atom attached), except that one of the hydrogens is replaced by an amine group, which is nitrogen with two hydrogen atoms attached. Perkin was trying to produce synthetic quinine, a plant substance used to fight the disease malaria. Perkin failed, but while experimenting, he created a purple dye. Called aniline purple, it was the first synthetic dye. Until that time, clothing was dyed with a few natural dyes from plants.

Seeing the possibilities, Perkin developed a way to make aniline dyes in many colors and in commercial quantities. Soon the world was using a variety of bright, permanent, synthetic dyes. Oddly, aniline itself has no color.

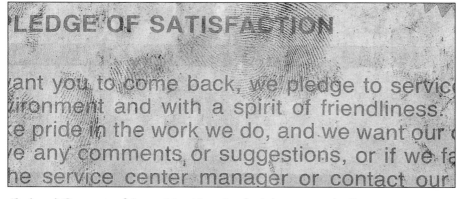

PLEDGE OF SATISFACTION

...ant you to come back, we pledge to servic...
...ironment and with a spirit of friendliness...
...e pride in the work we do, and we want our...
...e any comments, or suggestions, or if we fa...
...he service center manager or contact our...

Federal Bureau of Investigation technicians used nitrogen compounds to develop latent, or invisible, fingerprints on this business document. Latent prints are prints that cannot be seen until they are brought out by chemicals.

Exposing a Criminal

Fingerprints are often found on furniture and glassware—in other words, on smooth, hard surfaces. But fingerprints can also be discovered on paper and paper products by dipping the item in a solution of silver nitrate ($AgNO_3$). When exposed to light, the silver compound decomposes, leaving a brownish print that can be photographed.

Nitric acid is used by crime investigators to determine if a specific person has fired a gun recently, or even been in the vicinity of a gun when it went off. The primer (or detonator) in a bullet fired by a gun contains antimony (SB, element #51) and barium (Ba, element #56). In a Gunshot Primer Residue Test, a suspect's hands are swabbed with a 5-percent solution of nitric acid. Several different methods then might be used to reveal the amount of antimony or barium on the skin. These elements are usually found within 3 meters (10 ft) of a gun blast.

Nitrogen in Brief

Name: nitrogen, from Greek words meaning "niter former"; also called *azote*, meaning "lifeless," by the French

Symbol: N

Discoverers: Credit is usually given to Scottish chemist Daniel Rutherford, who recognized that there was another gas left in air after oxygen and carbon dioxide were driven off, but he did not regard it as an element. Proof of that was left to Lord Rayleigh in the 1870s.

Atomic number: 7

Atomic weight: 14.0067

Electron in the shells: 2, 5

Group: 15 (also called 5A); other elements in this group with 5 electrons in the outer shell include phosphorus, arsenic, antimony, and bismuth.

Usual characteristics: nonmetallic, odorless, colorless gas

Density (mass per unit volume): 1.251 kg per cubic meter of N_2 at 0°C (32°F) temperature at 1 atmosphere of pressure

Melting point (freezing point): –209.9°C (–345.8°F); higher for N_2

Boiling point (liquefaction point): –196°C (–321°F); lower for N_2

Abundance:

   Universe: 6th in abundance; however, it is only one of many elements totaling only 1.1% of the atoms in the universe

   Earth: One of many elements that together add up to only 1.4%

   Earth's crust: 19 parts per million; 33rd in abundance among the elements, it is one of many elements that together make up only 0.9% of Earth's crust

   Earth's atmosphere: Most abundant (78.1%)

   Human body: about 12% dry weight

Stable isotopes (nitrogen atoms with a different number of neutrons): there are two stable isotopes of nitrogen in nature: N-14 (99.64%) and N-15 (0.366%)

Radioactive isotopes: N-12, N-13, N-16, N-17, and N-18

Glossary

acid: definitions vary, but basically an acid is a corrosive substance that gives up a positive hydrogen ion, H^+, equal to a proton, when dissolved in water; indicates less than 7 on the pH scale because of its large number of hydrogen ions

alchemy: the combination of science, religion, and magic that preceded chemistry

alkali: a substance, such as a hydroxide or carbonate of an alkali metal, that when dissolved in water causes an increase in the hydroxide ion (OH^-) concentration, thus forming a basic solution.

anion: an ion with a negative charge

atom: the smallest amount of an element that exhibits the properties of the element, consisting of protons, electrons, and (usually) neutrons

base: a substance that accepts a hydrogen ion, H^+, when dissolved in water; indicates higher than 7 on the pH scale because of its small number of hydrogen ions

boiling point: the temperature at which a liquid at normal pressure evaporates into a gas, or a solid changes directly (sublimes) into a gas; also, the temperature at which a gas condenses into a liquid or solid

bond: the attractive force linking atoms together in a molecule

catalyst: a substance that causes or speeds a chemical reaction without itself being used up or consumed in the reaction

cation: an ion with a positive charge

chemical reaction: a transformation or change in a substance involving the electrons of the chemical elements making up the substance

combustion: burning, or rapid combination of a substance with oxygen, usually producing heat and light

compound: a substance formed by two or more chemical elements bound together by chemical means

covalent bond: a link between two atoms made by the atoms sharing electrons

crystal: a solid substance in which the atoms are arranged in three-dimensional patterns that create smooth outer surfaces, or faces

decompose: to break down a substance into its components

density: the amount of material in a given volume, or space; mass per unit volume; often stated as grams per cubic centimeter (g/cm^3)

diatomic: made up of two atoms

dissolve: to spread evenly throughout the volume of another substance

distillation: the process in which a liquid is heated until it evaporates and the gas is collected and condensed back into a liquid in another container; often used to separate mixtures into their different components

DNA: deoxyribonucleic acid, a chemical in the nucleus of each living cell, which carries genetic information

double bond: the sharing of two pairs of electrons between two atoms in a molecule

electrode: a device such as a metal plate that conducts electrons into or out of a solution or battery

element: a substance that cannot be split chemically into simpler substances that maintain the same characteristics; each of the 103 naturally occurring chemical elements is made up of atoms of the same kind

enzyme: one of many complex proteins that act as biological catalysts in the body

evaporate: to change from a liquid to a gas

fix: to change atmospheric nitrogen into nitrogen ions that can be utilized by a plant

fossil fuel: petroleum, natural gas, or coal, all of which are formed from the remains of plants and animals

gas: a state of matter in which the atoms or molecules move freely, matching the shape and volume of the container holding it

group: a vertical column in the Periodic Table, with each element having similar physical and chemical characteristics; also called chemical family

half-life: the period of time required for half of a radioactive element to decay

hormone: any of the various secretions of the endocrine glands that control different functions of the body, especially at the cellular level

hydrocarbon: a compound made of only carbon and hydrogen

inert: unlikely to react chemically

inorganic: not containing carbon

ion: an atom or molecule that has acquired an electric charge by gaining or losing one or more electrons

isotope: an atom with a different number of neutrons in its nucleus from other atoms of the same element

mass number: the total of protons and neutrons in the nucleus of an atom

melting point: the temperature at which a solid becomes a liquid, or a liquid changes to a solid

metal: a chemical element that conducts electricity, usually shines, or reflects light, is dense, and can be shaped; about three-quarters of the naturally occurring elements are metals

metalloid: a chemical element that has some characteristics of a metal and some of a nonmetal; includes some elements in groups 13 through 17 in the Periodic Table

molecule: the smallest amount of a substance that has the characteristics of the substance and consists of two or more atoms

monomer: a molecule that can be linked to many other identical molecules to make a polymer

neutral: 1) having neither acidic nor basic properties; 2) having no electrical charge

neutron: a subatomic particle within the nucleus of all atoms except hydrogen; has no electric charge

nonmetal: a chemical element that does not conduct electricity, is not dense, and is too brittle to be worked; nonmetals easily form ions, and they include some elements in groups 14 through 17 and all of group 18 in the Periodic Table

nucleus: 1) the central part of an atom, which has a positive electrical charge from its one or more protons; the nuclei of all atoms except hydrogen also include electrically neutral neutrons; 2) the central portion of most living cells that controls the activities of the cells and contains the genetic material

organic: containing carbon

oxidation: the loss of electrons during a chemical reaction, which occurs in conjunction with reduction; need not necessarily involve the element oxygen

pH: a measure of the acidity of a substance, on a scale of 0 to 14, with 7 being neutral; pH stands for "potential of hydrogen"

photosynthesis: in green plants, the process by which carbon dioxide and water, in the presence of light, are turned into sugars

pressure: the force exerted by an object divided by the area over which the force is exerted. The air at sea level exerts a pressure of 1,013 millibars (14.7 pounds per square inch), also called atmospheric pressure

protein: a complex biological chemical made by the linking of many amino acids

proton: a subatomic particle within the nucleus of all atoms; has a positive electric charge

radical: an atom or molecule that contains an unpaired electron

radioactive: spontaneously emitting high-energy particles

reduction: the gain of electrons during a chemical reaction; occurs in conjunction with oxidation

respiration: the process of taking in oxygen and giving off carbon dioxide

shell: a region surrounding the nucleus of an atom in which one or more electrons can occur. The inner shell can hold a maximum of two electrons; others may hold eight or more. If an atom's outer, or valence, shell does not hold its maximum number of electrons, the atom is subject to chemical reactions

solution: a mixture in which one substance is evenly distributed throughout another

sublime: to change directly from a solid to a gas without becoming a liquid first

synthetic: created artificially instead of occurring naturally

triple bond: the sharing of three pairs of electrons between two atoms in a molecule

ultraviolet: electromagnetic radiation which has a wavelength shorter than visible light

valence electron: an electron located in the outer shell of an atom, available to participate in chemical reactions

For Further Information

BOOKS

Atkins, P. W. *The Periodic Kingdom: A Journey into the Land of the Chemical Elements.* NY: Basic Books, 1995

Heiserman, David L. *Exploring Chemical Elements and Their Compounds.* Blue Ridge Summit, PA: Tab Books, 1992

Hoffman, Roald, and Vivian Torrence. *Chemistry Imagined: Reflections on Science.* Washington, DC: Smithsonian Institution Press, 1993

Newton, David E. *Chemical Elements.* Venture Books. Danbury, CT: Franklin Watts, 1994

Yount, Lisa. *Antoine Lavoisier: Founder of Modern Chemistry.* "Great Minds of Science" series. Springfield, NJ: Enslow Publishers, 1997

CD-ROM

Discover the Elements: The Interactive Periodic Table of the Chemical Elements. Paradigm Interactive, Greensboro, NC, 1995

INTERNET SITES

Note that useful sites on the Internet can change and even disappear. If the following site addresses do not work, use a search engine that you find useful, such as Yahoo:

> http://www.yahoo.com

or AltaVista:

> http://altavista.digital.com

A very thorough listing of the major characteristics, uses, and compounds of all the chemical elements can be found at a site called WebElements:

> http://www.shef.ac.uk/~chem/web-elements/

A Canadian site on the Nature of the Environment includes a large section on the elements in the various Earth systems:

> http://www.cent.org/geo12/geo12/htm

Colored photos of various molecules, cells, and biological systems can be viewed at:

> http://www.clarityconnect.com/webpages/-cramer/PictureIt/welcome.htm

Many subjects are covered on WWW Virtual Library. It also includes a useful collection of links to other sites:

> http://www.earthsystems.org/Environment/shtml

INDEX